THE R.E.W.R.I.T.E. METHOD

THE PARENT AND EDUCATOR GUIDE FOR GETTING MIDDLE SCHOOLERS TO FALL IN LOVE WITH WRITING

By
T.D. Flenaugh

Published by Writertai LLC
Printed in the United States
Cover Design by TD Flenaugh
ISBN 979-8-9887076-7-7

First published in the United States of America.

ACKNOWLEDGMENTS

The following organizations and institutions have bolstered me as a teacher and a professional by continuously challenging me to improve and giving me creative license to form curriculum and activities that motivate me – and more importantly – the students I serve.

- The UCLA Writing Project (UCLAWP)
- The California Writing Project
- The National Writing Project
- National Board Certification
- UCLAWP Writers Anonymous founded by Jane Hancock
- My once-upon-a-time writing group: Amy, Michelle, Sarah, and Elizabeth at the University of Southern California Masters of Professional Writing Program.
- My beloved writing partner, Jemila Pratt.
- My beloved planning partner, Charmaine Jackson Gilmore.
- My daughter, Nia Pia, who is my purpose.

DISCLAIMER

The advice contained in this book might not be suitable for everyone. The author designed the information to present her opinion about the subject matter. The reader must carefully investigate all aspects of any decision before committing. The author obtained the information contained herein from sources she believes to be reliable and from her personal experience, but she neither implies nor intends any guarantee.

The author particularly disclaims any liability, loss, or risk taken by individuals who directly or indirectly act on the information contained herein. The author believes the advice presented here is sound, but readers cannot hold her responsible for either their actions or the risk taken by individuals who directly or indirectly act on the information contained herein.

TABLE OF CONTENTS

INTRODUCTION

I am TD Flenaugh, a lifelong educator who supports parents in teaching their children how to unlock the power of education to ensure the next generation has the skills and knowledge to advance their family legacy.

As a parent, you may have coaxed, encouraged, or even threatened your children to take education seriously. You might be on the verge of giving up and accepting that they are not "into" school.

You may have a different issue. Your child is ready to go and eager to learn, but you must figure out how and what to teach them to move them to the next level. You believe the previous writing instruction at your child's school is subpar, or maybe you are a homeschool parent who needs to step up the writing curriculum.

Depending on the stage of her life, I had the same issues with my daughter. As she grew, I knew education would give her the advantages she needed to thrive, but I didn't know how to hook her into learning. I became a teacher when my daughter was four years old. Through trial and error, I figured out how to get her to love learning, as well as many of my family members and students.

I created this book because I have met too many parents who allowed their children to fail in the school system because they gave over their power to teachers and the school system. Many mothers and fathers told me the year their child was deprived of a quality education. If it was the second grade teacher, their children's educational gaps still existed five years later. I wrote this book because parents must remember their power.

You are the first teachers and the continuous teachers. I want parents and caregivers to take back the reins, and stop leaving their children's education to teachers. Most educators are temporary fixtures in your child's life and often come from different ways of understanding and knowing. This book will help parents facilitate their children's journey to unlocking a love for writing - a keystone skill in achieving their goals.

The R.E.W.R.I.T.E. Method is a guide to help teachers and parents (a child's first and continuous teachers) to get their middle schoolers to fall in love with writing. Children do not come with handbooks, but this book will show you how to unearth your child's genius and cultivate a lifelong love for learning.

I learned these lessons from my personal life as a writer, as a mother, and as a teacher.

Growing up as a sensitive child, I journaled to untangle my thoughts. Once on paper, I could fully examine those dilemmas and issues that had occupied my brain. It allowed me to objectively analyze those issues and construct peace. I could reflect on it, and I could grow. Those journals served as evidence of my growth.

As a girl, I loved to pour out the frustrations and challenges like the writers I experienced as a hungry young reader. But that emotion was squashed by my parents' embarrassment. I wrote honestly about my feelings and my perspective, and it gave me catharsis; however, the highly critical environment formed by my parents' shame stunted me.

Whenever I wrote something, my mom focused on the negative or incorrect parts:

"What does that say?"

"It does not even make sense."

I soaked up that negativity and internalized the message that I could not write well. Dealing with this made me hide my writing. I still wrote down everything I went through as a child, though.

Later, I used my writing skills to apply for fifty scholarships and win thousands of dollars. As a young mother, I used writing to build a life for me and my daughter.

You may have budding writers who put your business out in the streets. On the other hand, the reverse may be true. Your kids may have decided they hate writing. Either way, it is not easy.

I have figured out a productive process through my teaching and parenting experiences. Now you can access my method to assist your child in cutting through the struggle and begin to view themselves as writers - all through joyful experiences. Here is an overview of the REWRITE Method:

Root causes and recognizing talents
Effective Feedback
Writing Process
Real World Purposes
Intentional Practice
Traits
Encourage creativity

Root causes and recognizing talents

The R stands for root causes and recognizing talents. We know many children do not love writing, but why? This chapter suggests different hindrances that prevent your child from writing progress.

We must also recognize talents. A child's writing strengths will fortify their identity as a writer, and provide the frame needed to construct strong writing skills.

Effective Feedback

Instead of focusing on negative aspects of children's writing, build them up through a balance of positive feedback, questioning, and corrective feedback. This chapter gives detailed methods for keeping children open to learning despite errors and misunderstandings.

Writing Process

Although many teachers have a specific procedure for navigating the writing process taught to students, it is important that students develop their own sequence for approaching written tasks. We will define various phases of the writing process and explain how to guide students toward adopting their own unique procedure.

Real World Purposes

We know that children respond to relevance. Writing tasks should relate to their daily lives, future endeavors, and responsibilities. I encourage you to look into the wild world of literature and media to develop prompts and tasks to connect children to the functionality of writing.

Intentional Practice

As children get older, it is important to know exactly what is required and support children in reaching these goals. This chapter details how to develop a writing practice that nurtures continuous growth.

Traits

Traits represent different elements of writing. Each area provides a concept tied to specific skill development. These concrete terms refer to specific aspects of writing. The traits are conventions, organization, word choice, ideas, sentences, voice, and publishing.

Encourage creativity

The REWRITE Method suggests ways to lean into imagination and critical thinking by using mentor texts, avoiding negativity about writing, and providing the freedom of choice.

R FOR ROOT CAUSES AND RECOGNIZING TALENTS

1

In the journey to help your middle schooler embrace writing, it is crucial to identify and address the underlying issues that may be causing their aversion to this essential skill. In this chapter, we delve into the various reasons a child might dislike writing and provide guidance on how parents can play a pivotal role in finding solutions.

COMMON ROOT CAUSES

1. Difficulty with Fine Motor Skills: Some young writers struggle with the physical aspect of writing, such as correctly holding a pencil or pen. Fine motor skills refer to the ability to move or use the small muscles in our hands and fingers. Observe your child while holding a pencil to notice any challenges in gripping a pencil, pen, or typing. Usually, these movements come naturally, and many of us rarely think of these movements. These challenges can turn writing into a frustrating and daunting task. Exercises may strengthen and develop the coordination of these muscles. In other situations, permanent support may be necessary. For some, occupational therapy or ergonomic writing tools may be sufficient in making writing more manageable.

2. Lack of Confidence: Self-doubt hinders a child's writing journey. If your child does not trust their writing abilities, they may shy away from writing. Encouragement, positive feedback, and constructive praise will boost their confidence and motivate them to write more enthusiastically.

3. Learning Differences or Disabilities: Some children have specific learning differences or disabilities like dyslexia or dysgraphia, making writing particularly challenging. Identifying these conditions and seeking professional support -- such as special education services -- can help your child overcome these hurdles and develop a more positive attitude towards writing.

4. Dyslexia: According to the National Institutes of Health, dyslexia is "a brain-based learning disability that specifically impairs a person's ability to read." Writers with dyslexia often have the following characteristics: "a high percentage of misspelled words, difficult-to-read handwriting, poor organization, a lack of fully developed ideas, and a lack of diverse vocabulary." (NIH 2018)

5. Dysgraphia: When parents and teachers see sloppy writing, we often associate it with laziness or failure to focus on the details needed to write neatly. It may be a symptom of a more serious issue. Dysgraphia is a neurological disorder that causes a person's writing to be distorted, rendering it sloppy or illegible.

6. Lack of Interest: Writing becomes enjoyable when a child is passionate about the topic. It is crucial to discover your child's interests and encourage them to write about subjects that captivate their attention. Providing diverse reading materials and exposing them to various writing genres will also stimulate their interest in writing.

7. Past Experiences: Negative situations can scar a child's perception of their ability to improve as a writer. As parents, it is essential to position mistakes as opportunities for growth, thus creating a safe and supportive writing environment. Celebrate successes and encourage youngsters to view setbacks as stepping stones toward improvement.

8. Limited Exposure: Children with limited exposure to different types of writing may need help understanding the purpose and benefits of composition. Parents can expand their children's horizons by introducing them to various writing styles, from creative storytelling to persuasive essays. This exposure can help children appreciate the versatility and power of the written word.

The sacred parent-child relationship positions caregivers to uncover the root causes of their child's writing difficulties. A deep understanding of a child's strengths, weaknesses, and interests enables you to tailor solutions that will transform their antagonistic relationship with writing into a positive and fulfilling one. Addressing these underlying issues and fostering an environment of encouragement and support can help cultivate a lifelong love for the written word in middle schoolers.

RECOGNIZING WRITING TALENTS

Knowing your child's writing strengths will help you nurture their existing skills and boost their belief in their ability to improve. In the REWRITE Method, one of the key pillars is building upon your child's current abilities.

When we embark on this writing journey with children, we need to highlight how their unique personality shines through their words -

whether written or spoken. Everyone has the potential to become a proficient writer, but it all starts with recognizing how they already excel.

Here are some questions to help you identify those key talents:

- Are they naturally funny?
- Do they have a knack for pointing out intriguing aspects of things in a unique way?
- Do they often say phrases that make them stand out?
- Do they incorporate advanced words into their speech?
- Can they describe things in a captivating way?

Work with what children already have. Start at that sweet spot just a bit beyond what they already know. The Zone of Proximal Development refers to beginning instruction at moderate difficulty, something that is not too easy but not too hard for them to grasp.

As you discover these strengths, you will begin to notice weaknesses. Do not dwell on them or point out every mistake to your child. Start by focusing on their strengths because you want to bolster their confidence. The ultimate goal is for them to fall in love with writing. Try not to fixate on correctness. It is common to want to correct spelling, capitalization, and punctuation, but do not let that divert your focus at the beginning of this process.

Emphasize their strengths. The REWRITE Method does not ignore weaknesses, but it is vital to highlight where they excel. When the time comes to work on areas of improvement, they will be more receptive. Picture a seesaw where you can tip the balance toward positivity by emphasizing their strengths. Doing this helps our students establish a positive relationship with writing.

UNCOVER YOUR CHILD'S WRITING POTENTIAL!

If a child's writing shows limited promise, look outside of their writing. Your child may excel in spoken expression. Notice if they speak passionately, use highly expressive words, or employ figurative language.

Closely observe the things they say. If necessary, jot it down. Use their spoken words as evidence to demonstrate their writing potential. Encourage them to write down their words, highlighting their capacity to become a fantastic writer by showcasing their mastery of language and knack for turning a phrase.

CHAPTER 1 REVIEW - R FOR ROOT CAUSES AND RECOGNIZING TALENTS

This chapter urges parents and educators to delve into the reasons behind a child's reluctance towards writing. Understanding root causes is key to addressing any aversion. Sometimes, it might be as straightforward as adjusting the balance between praise and constructive feedback. However, it could also be more intricate, stemming from physical impediments or neurological conditions. Identifying these underlying factors is crucial as it guides the selection of appropriate activities aimed at cultivating writing proficiency.

Additionally, it is essential to acknowledge and appreciate your child's inherent talents. Take note of their talents – perhaps it is their ability to articulate thoughts verbally or their distinct speech patterns. Encourage them to incorporate these natural strengths into their writing.

E FOR EFFECTIVE FEEDBACK

2

Whenever my daughter would face harassment and name-calling, I would hold her and tell her she was beautiful. I told her those other kids were jealous, so they needed to put someone else down. She would wiggle away from me. "You're my mom. You have to say those things."

My motherly pep talks exemplified ineffective feedback. My daughter soaked in the negativity of others because it was what she heard most often; it rang in her head and echoed inside her body. They pointed out specific parts of her they thought worthy of ridicule.

Instead of giving her general positive feedback, I learned to give her specific praise based on her long hair, her curvy shape, and her shapely lips. Going further, I gave her compliments highlighting her personality, like her humor, kindness, and creativity. When feedback is specific, it becomes real. We can look at, touch it, and use it as evidence.

In the same way, writing feedback must be specific and consistent. The delivery can build up or break down self-esteem. We must give it time to soak into our children's hearts and minds. That happens when we couple habitual practice and positive feedback. The consistency supplies children with evidence of their writing magic. They can flip back the pages or open old files to evaluate how much they have grown in their ability to craft the written word.

Instead, many teachers and parents focus on the weak areas of a young person's writing - sloppiness, incorrect spelling, and skipped words. Parents who have not been paying attention to their child's writing might be alarmed to find that it is crap. Do not be surprised! There may be some exceptions; a few families will be pleasantly surprised. But most will not.

Do not get distracted by the quality. Remember to build them up through noticing and marking areas of strength so they can begin to recognize what they do well. In turn, they will be open to work on improvements if they view themselves as solid writers who need a few tweaks to improve.

Even if children are on grade level, their writing will not be at adult level. Principles of the REWRITE Method will bridge the gap between their base level and grade level proficiency.

Have You Had These Challenges?

- Your child hides their writing in fear of what others may say.
- Their writing does not make any sense.
- Your child's writing is littered with mistakes.

REFRAME MISTAKES

Reframe how you and your child view mistakes. Do not take them personally. As a teacher-mama, I remember I had to check myself. I was much more understanding of my students in class when they made mistakes. I accepted them at their level. For my daughter, I felt upset when she made certain errors. Before I learned better, I felt her writing stumbles were a poor reflection of me. I commanded her to redo it, and scolded her for not being careful with her work. I had to fix this approach and repair the damage.

Reframing mistakes will eventually change how children deal with setbacks and their shortcomings. Let children know they may not understand a concept or new technique the first time. Share with them the many times you tried and failed before finally mastering different skills.

4 POSITIVE TO 1 IMPROVEMENT RATIO

Fight the urge to fix all of their writing mistakes. To inspire young writers, compliment their work. Four positive compliments should be noted before providing a suggestion for improvement.

Even if you cannot read it, prepare a few compliments:

1. "Looks like you worked hard on this. Why don't you go ahead and read your writing to me."
2. "This is such a thoughtful gesture! Your grandma will really love this."
3. "Wow! You wrote an entire page!"
4. "I really liked when you wrote this line: (read the line). It was very _____ (touching, funny, etc.)!"

Here are a few more ideas to note areas of strength: high-level vocabulary, use of sensory details, and correct capitalization.

Think back to when children learned to walk; we had to let them fall so that they could master walking. Our job was to provide the soft carpeting they could fall on without hurting themselves. On the journey of learning to write well, we need to provide encouragement and cheers to buoy youngsters as they undergo the steps, falls, and mistakes fundamental to the journey of learning to write well.

AREAS OF IMPROVEMENT

You should know that when kids challenge themselves to incorporate high-level vocabulary and use sophisticated sentence structures, the number of errors increases. It is developmentally appropriate to notice many stumbles as they try a more complex level of writing.

Common Areas of Improvement

- Lack of paragraphing
- Commonly confused words
- Missing punctuation
- Confusion or lack of capitalization rules
- Run-on sentences
- Redundant or wordy writing

When children write a full page of work or several paragraphs of a composition, it is normal for there to be at least thirty mistakes. As a beginning teacher, I have spent hours marking up students' papers. I made sure to mark every mistake. I thought they would notice the mistakes and improve. The result: students returned their work with the same mistakes, but at least it was neater. You are not going to be able to address all thirty errors effectively. Correcting too many mistakes at a time can be overwhelming and discouraging. Children need lessons and extended practice that allows them to understand why you marked their paper and how to make the changes.

HOW TO ADDRESS AREAS OF IMPROVEMENT MINI-LESSONS

When your child has never heard of or has limited knowledge about a concept or skill, provide a mini-lesson. Mini-lessons refer to a short (10-minutes or less) sequence of activities to introduce a skill. In the case of paragraphing, your student may write a whole block of text that spans a full page or more without any paragraph breaks.

Teach them how to organize their writing into separate paragraphs. Provide the students with clear rules, such as the list below for separating paragraphs in a narrative:

When there is a new speaker, start a new paragraph.

If there is a new location

A new time of day

A new day.

The need for a mini-lesson also arises when someone makes the same type of mistake repeatedly. For example, they may continuously confuse words. Maybe they keep using the word wander and wonder incorrectly. Demonstrate several ways to use wonder and wander correctly in context.

1. Give them a quick explanation on the meanings.
   - Use an instructional video that explains the proper usage.

2. Use a writing piece that uses the target words correctly. Your child can infer the meaning from context. Explain how to identify the difference between the two.

3. Lift sentences from their writing, and deconstruct sentences to ensure they know how to correct it.

The detailed mini-lesson can be found in the REWRITE Workbook.

Tips on Revision (Improving the Writing Quality)

The first point of critique should be a suggestion for revision (instead of an edit or correction). For example, a writer can add sentences to create or describe a character's outfit.

Revision to improve word choice expands children's vocabulary and moves their writing into the next stratosphere of quality. When a student wrote a description of her baby sister, she used the phrase "baby sister" eight times. I showed her how to revise for word choice by spelling out the baby's name, using the word infant, and describing her as "the new bundle" or "the new member of the family." This demonstrates ways to be flexible with language. This activity is provided in detail in the REWRITE Workbook.

Here are a few more statements that suggest revisions:

1. Tell me more about what she/he was wearing.

2. Give three detailed sentences to describe the park. It sounded like a lot of fun.

3. What did your group do on the trip? What are three events that happened during the trip? Give us those details. I want to know more.

These suggestions for improvement do not feel critical. They extend what is already written, and stretch the writer toward strengthening their descriptive skills.

After addressing quality, we can focus on editing for correctness.

PEER REVIEW AND FEEDBACK TECHNIQUES

Team activities ignite a love for writing. Peer review happens when fellow students work together to read and review each other's work to get better at self-reflection, self-editing, and self-revision.

The Set-Up

1. Pair up two writers who will each come with a draft of their writing.
2. If the partners are new at peer review and feedback, we recommend starting with editing. Editing is the most manageable area to provide feedback.
3. Hone in on one type of error, such as capitalization. Provide them with a handout from the REWRITE Workbook that focuses on capitalization rules, which includes the questions below:
   - Do we have capital letters at the beginning of the sentence?
   - Have we capitalized the specific names of people?
   - Have we capitalized the specific names of places?
   - Have we incorrectly capitalized common objects or places?
   - Provide a Peer Review Checklist to guide students through the steps.

More about Peer Review Checklists

A key tool for peer review is to have a checklist. Checklists can be altered based on purpose. Sometimes, the checklist may be for editing.

Other times, revision is the purpose. We have several examples in the REWRITE Workbook. When kids are getting started, the focus should be narrow. Use a list that includes one type of edit or revision. For example, it may be word choice, specifically revising for repeated words. The result will be a more specific and more focused writing piece devoid of redundancies.

THE REWRITE METHOD PEER REVIEW

During peer review, ensure students hold on to their papers or documents. Some teachers ask student pairs to exchange papers or to allow editing access to electronic drafts, but the REWRITE Peer Review alters this practice.

Procedure for the REWRITE Peer Review Process:

1. Students keep their papers.
2. Partner A will read their paper aloud to their partner.
3. Partner B will ask Partner A questions about the partner's writing.
4. Partner A takes notes and marks up their paper based on questions from Partner B.

Reading the paper aloud allows them to hear what they wrote.

Reading Work Aloud leads to Self-editing & Revising

When students read their writing aloud, their mouth has to form each word and enable them to hear each word. In this way, they can catch those mistakes. The brain will correct a writer's work when reading it silently. Our fingers — whether writing or typing — move slower than our brains. I remind students that one hundred percent of the time, they will find mistakes in their writing because the brain is on word eight, while the writing fingers may be on word number three. Developing authors can notice repeated words and phrases. They can also catch that the wording in some parts do not quite fit. This method nurtures independence because students will eventually be able to identify low quality.

BENEFITS OF THE PARTNER IN PEER REVIEW

Writers operate from their memories. Once the reader shares aloud with someone, the partner can ask questions to fill in gaps in events and details.

When a peer asks questions, they can offer feedback on missing information from the audience's perspective. The writer will naturally miss these areas because it is clear in their minds.

Below is an excerpt from a conversation from a peer review session after the partner asked a question about an inconsistency in the sequence:

"I didn't even explain that part. My baby sister came back home four days later. My mom went to the hospital, and four days later, my baby sister and Mama came home. I did not even put that part there."

During the peer review process, make adjustments so students can remain in control. They can sit side by side with a peer and follow the checklist. Remember that the checklist should have a narrow focus, such as capitalization, ending punctuation, or sentence starters. The student reading their work retains control of the writing utensil or keyboard. They should be the only one marking and making changes to their writing. The partner gives suggestions.

The writer decides whether to heed the reviewer's feedback. They may choose to leave their writing unchanged. Kids must develop their voice through personal preference. The REWRITE Method keeps the author in the driver's seat during peer review. Of course, they will earn a grade or score based on meeting specific criteria. As far as creative control, they have it! Let them keep it.

CHAPTER 2 REVIEW - E FOR EFFECTIVE FEEDBACK

Make detailed, positive feedback a habit that nurtures your child's writing confidence. Brace yourself! It is normal for young writers to have horrible writing. There will be dozens of mistakes, but this chapter prepares parents and educators to focus on what they do well, using a 4-to-1 ratio of positive to negative comments. Do not shame children for their writing mistakes. Let go of any shame associated with your children's writing level.

When reviewing their work, look for a repeated type of mistake that will improve several parts of their writing. Isolated mistakes will lead to nitpicking their work. This approach heightens the child's awareness of these specific errors, enabling them to rectify these across multiple sections of their work. Common errors are lack of paragraphing, missing ending punctuation, run-on sentences, misunderstanding capitalization rules, as well as redundancies in words and ideas.

Teach children how to fix their errors through short bursts of learning with mini-lessons. A brief series of activities that explain the reasoning behind an error and how to remedy this kind of misstep will lead to internalizing the concept so that the child will be able to self-correct errors in the future.

Through peer editing and review, young writers will read their own work aloud to build self-efficacy with checklists that provide guidelines for independently improving their compositions.

By consistently employing these strategies, parents and educators can effectively nurture children's ability to compose, fostering an environment where young writers can flourish.

W FOR WRITING PROCESS

3

E ach individual develops their own writing process. You read that correctly. While teachers lead students through stages systematically, it is not a rigid system. Deviation is allowed, although it may not be encouraged by some educators. As a writer myself, I understand that writing is an extension of each individual's thinking, which makes it distinctive to each person. Since teachers are temporary fixtures in children's lives, we work to give students tools they can follow long after we part ways. Reaching the pinnacle of writing ability means owning the process.

Proficient writers unlock the right sequence as an individual to unleash their signature voice. Let your child in on this secret. Some writers list ideas first, while others start brainstorming on a word web. Still others prefer to begin drafting immediately.

Help your child develop their own plan of action to complete any written task. We will define various phases of the writing process and explain how to guide students to independently progress through each phase.

Have you had these challenges?

- I do not know what to write
- I do not like writing
- Children write a few sentences and say they do not have any more ideas.
- Your child cannot understand why they need to do more than one draft.

Middle schoolers need adult guidance through the writing process. By the publishing stage, kids should have completed each step in the process.

The right combination of moves will reveal the beauty and wonder of writing. That does not always happen because of how writing is taught in a very prescriptive way. Even how you have established yourself as a writer may have blocked you from helping your child get to a place where they construct their own worlds.

WRITING PROCESS STAGES

Prewriting

Prewriting, in which students generate ideas, usually happens before sentences and paragraphs. It may include a combination of the following:

- drawing
- listing
- making notes on graphic organizers
- creating outlines

In the prewriting phase, kids brainstorm, list ideas, and build a graphic organizer with phrases and words. For example, they may create a circle map, or just list information about a topic in short phrases. There may not be any organization during this stage.

Another level of prewriting is an outline or structured thinking, such as a tree map or a cause-and-effect map, where they organize ideas.

Drafting or Rough Draft

In the drafting phase, writers form ideas into sentences and paragraphs using the prewriting – graphic organizers or brainstorming notes. A rough draft or sloppy copy should consist of several paragraphs. Fix any errors in conventions (grammar, usage, mechanics, spelling, and capitalization) in later phases. Focus on getting ideas down in sentences and paragraphs.

Revising

Revision involves improving the quality of writing:

- adding details
- choosing more precise or vivid words
- rearranging sentences for clarity and flow

Consider the two sentences below. Which one is the better sentence for a middle schooler?

Sentence A: I have a red shirt.

Sentence B: As I moved through the hollway, my selky scarlit blose feel smooth against my skin.

Sentence Analysis: A second grader could have written Sentence A. Sentence B has sensory details, names a sophisticated color, and has a specific shirt type. Sentence A is a correct sentence with kindergarten-level writing quality. The second sentence demonstrates a higher level of complexity.

One sentence is correct, but it is low-level. The other sentence, in turn, has many errors in grammar and spelling, but it is a higher-quality sentence. It has a more sophisticated vocabulary and complexity. It is not a correct sentence, but middle schoolers should produce sentences with grade-level vocabulary and varied sentence structures.

In the process of reaching for more sophistication and varied sentences, an increase in mistakes are typical. A simple sentence like "My cat is yellow" only uses high-frequency words from primary grades. We must expect more from our children, or they will not be ready for high school advanced placement courses, the rigors of college, or to produce proficient correspondence to navigate career and personal business. As middle school kids challenge themselves to improve vocabulary and use a variety of sentence structures, reassure them that making mistakes is a natural part of the learning process.

EDITING PHASE

After revision, focus on correcting the mistakes. In the editing phase, support students with internalizing the acronym G.U.M.S.- C: Grammar, Usage, Mechanics, Spelling, and Capitalization.

G for Grammar

Have we followed grammar rules? Follow formal English language rules, subject-verb agreement, and singular verb-noun agreement.

U for Usage

involves using words appropriately in context, meaning they know how to correctly use frequently confused words.

Commonly Confused Words

- they're and their
- you're and your
- too, to, two
- specific and Pacific (Ocean)

M for Mechanics

Mechanics is a fancy word for punctuation - periods, question marks, exclamation points, commas, and quotation marks. It is common for students to form sentences that continue for several lines without punctuation. Help them find sentence breaks by locating words that extend the sentence. For example, many students use the phrase "and then" to keep a run-on going. Show children how to break the sentences into simple, compound, and complex sentences to improve clarity and flow. Other mechanics lessons can focus on how to insert quotation marks or commas to correct their writing.

S for spelling

Check to see if the writing follows spelling rules. Check spelling by using word processing platforms like Google Docs and Microsoft Word. Help them navigate the use of electronic tools.

Prompt students to self-check by asking, "What words are misspelled?" At this point, the kids should know how to use a spell checker or look up words online. Do not shame them if they do not know how to use it. Show them instead. Give them the confidence to use words they know even when they do not know how to spell them. When students message online and text more often using informal language, they communicate without spelling words letter by letter.

C represents capitalization

Many students have the habit of using all lowercase letters. Some are really out of practice because of the audience. They are usually writing text messages to friends. They disregard grammar and spelling rules during informal text and online messaging conversations. In certain spaces, that is acceptable and even preferred. When we need formal or academic writing, we want to ensure they follow capitalization rules. Even teenagers may have problems with capitalization because of texting and writing online – situations that do not require following rules.

PUBLISHING PHASE

Publishing involves any method for making the writing public. As children progress through the writing process, help them focus on an audience for their work when they finish.

Scaffolding the Writing Process - *Providing scaffolds will aid students in completing their work.* Not all students will be able to progress through the writing process - at first. Special supports called scaffolds may need to be in place **temporarily** to ensure they can complete their work. For example, drafting sentences and paragraphs may be too challenging - in the beginning.

Do not resort to permanent scaffolding. Children will not be prepared to let the supports go when it is time for state tests and other assessments. Teachers and parents will eventually believe that our students cannot function without them.

This is a FALLACY! Our children are intelligent and capable. We must give them the expectation and the opportunity to show what they know.

Anything less is a disservice! Here are are few ideas to assist young writers:

Inform children of their expected outcomes - Students need to know what average middle schoolers should be able to produce. Lowering the amount or quality of their work without informing them of the standard, disadvantages students. I have witnessed many children who think that they are doing wonderfully because they have grown comfortable completing scaffolded work. They are not striving for more because they forgot the high standard they need to meet, or they were never told of the level of work they should be able to perform. Before providing scaffolds, inform kids that it is temporary support until they can produce work to the level of the standard requirements. Then remind them every time the scaffold is used.

Sentence frames - This scaffold involves providing children with the beginning words of a sentence. Heavy scaffolding may have up to five words, so that a student only needs to add one or two words.

Partially filled out outlines - Outlines provide the paragraph by paragraph structure of a multiple paragraph response. Scaffold by detailing what should be the focus of each paragraph. Heavy scaffolds can include a focus and details for the sentences in each paragraph.

Removing scaffolds - Regularly inform students that the scaffolds are temporary, and slowly remove scaffolds. For example, if students need heavy support in forming sentences, start with five-word sentence frames for two weeks or less. Then for the next two weeks, move to three-word sentence frames that require students to write four or five words to complete the sentence. Then move to two-word sentence frames for two weeks. Finally, they will not need sentence frames any longer. Follow the same gradual removal schedule for outlines and any other supports.

When we teach kids to be more independent, we must give them systems and strategies. This is why we use acronyms that name the steps and moves to guide a child through different stages of the writing process. For example, the acronym G.U.M.S.C. is discussed throughout this book to prompt students to edit or correct their work independently. The acronyms help them internalize how to improve their writing.

Let students know to remember the acronym because they will eventually need to use these skills without guidance. Teachers are not allowed to read directions during assessments. They provide an overview of what students will do on the test, but children must read prompts, texts, and directions for each specific task alone. Remind them that the acronyms are a way to remember what to do as they move through a task independently.

The REWRITE Workbook offers several outlines and sentence frame examples with varying degrees of scaffolding.

TIPS FOR IMPLEMENTATION

Avoid addressing corrections while drafting, which slows down students. Many youngsters hesitate while writing because they worry about being correct instead of expressing ideas. Encourage kids to focus on the quality and the message instead of accurate writing. Reinforce the practice of valuing ideas and thoughts over correctness.

Make distinctions between the various stages. Here are a few suggestions for how to make the phases different.

- Write the rough draft by hand

- Mark up the rough draft with notes (written in a different color) to note 5 revisions that will be made.
- Type the edited version.
- Require that the published version be copied into a new document with pictures or printed and decorated. Find a location for the published version (not just for the teacher). For example, the writing can be posted on a refrigerator, emailed to grandma, framed and hung in a parent's office, or published on a family website or social media page.

CHAPTER 3 REVIEW - W FOR THE WRITING PROCESS

In this chapter, we reviewed the stages of the writing process: prewriting, drafting, revising, editing, and publishing. Each stage of the process moves kids closer to a completed written product. As children mature, they will begin to identify their unique writing process. Supporting children as they move through the stages for various writing tasks will allow them to learn their preferences. Some will like to dive into drafting, while others will enjoy listing words and phrases on a graphic organizer. All of the stages line the pathway to higher development in writing.

Depending on their level, it may be a steep climb. Let them know you will be with them every step of the way. Help them (by providing scaffolds) and remind them that supports will be slowly removed. The goal is for them to independently read prompts, plan and decide on the focus of the paragraphs and ideas that need to fully answer, and proceed through the writing process with a multiple paragraph response.

R FOR REAL WORLD PURPOSES 4

N aturally stir up writing love by showing kids the power of written words throughout their world. Here are some familiar complaints that you may need to overcome:

- Writing is boring.
- What is the point of writing about this?
- The only person who will read this is the teacher.
- How am I going to use this as an adult?

To reframe negative attitudes toward writing, connect writing tasks to real life purposes. Be a model writer for your child and give students many opportunities to practice their writing.

PARENT AS WRITER

As a parent and adult, you constantly use writing skills. Allow kids to see you writing and model the writing process. Let youngsters know how you share your brilliance through writing. It could be a proposal to a new client, a billing dispute with a utility company, or a grant proposal.

Talk them through how you tackle writing tasks. Do you list ideas first, begin with a brainstorm on a word web, or start drafting immediately?

Explain the thinking behind your process. Flaunting your creativity will inspire children. Sharing inside information about your writing preferences will be pivotal in supporting them as they develop their writing process.

FAMILY LIFE AND WRITING

Practice builds self-efficacy, which happens with regular engagement. Here are a few ideas: creating lists, jotting notes, writing journals, and giving words as gifts. Let us delve deeper into these categories and how we can integrate writing into daily family life and your kids' world.

We know children respond to relevance. Writing tasks should relate to their daily lives, future endeavors, or current responsibilities. I encourage you to look into the wild world of literature and media to develop prompts and tasks that connect children to the functionality of writing and the satisfaction borne from being prepared.

Crafting the best prompts for a child requires that you are attuned to your children's changing desires and interests. It also requires you to provide choices.

Make writing a typical family activity - not just for school. There are dozens of daily writing tasks required of families outside of school. Think about what is needed to handle business and communicate. Which ones involve reading and writing? Begin by integrating children into these written tasks. As you work alongside your child to interact with the written word, you will collect information about their writing proficiency and help them gain confidence simultaneously. Ensure your child uses these activities regularly to increase capability.

Letter of Complaint

If your family received poor service at a restaurant, help your children compose a letter of complaint. Help them articulate the problems with their order and how the staff interacted with them. Support them in finding the names of owners or managers and how to address the letter to the establishment so the writing can get to the involved or responsible parties. Point out that this situation calls for formal writing. Explain that the receivers of the complaint may judge their writing and place value on the complaint based on their perception of intelligence, which may lead to the complaint being deemed unimportant or dismissed.

Letters of Accolades

If the whole family has a great experience on a boat, a ship, or a cruise, kids can write a letter about all the great activities and moments shared. Take the time to send it to the supervisor, showing kids how their writing can make an impact.

List Making

Another way to integrate writing into daily life includes lists. Lists support gradual independence. It is low stakes and short - just a few words at a time. Co-create lists for groceries and errands. List the places to go and itemize tasks for each location. After trying this a few times, you may want children to have a different list. In that case, create a separate parent and a kid list (a copycat list).

Teens can create evening and morning schedules to organize themselves and demonstrate their writing ability:

How long and when (specific times and length of time) will they spend on each task?

- Shower
- Personal hygiene (combing hair, moisturizing, or make-up)
- Getting dressed
- Breakfast
- Packing backpack (headphones, charger, laptop, books, folders, homework)
- Clothes preparation (ironing, folding, washing)

For a trip to the laundromat, list the loads, the quarters needed or money card, and the laundry detergent (or other cleaning agents like bleach).

A visit to the bank could require several tasks:

- deposit checks
- put saved coins in a counting machine
- get two rolls of quarters
- two money orders
- $200 cash for spending
- transfer money to savings
- order new checks
- payment on a loan

Middle schoolers should be able to write the list. Use it as an opportunity to observe their writing. Do they know the spelling of all sight words or high-frequency words they should know? If they do not, it is the perfect time to learn. Reassure them that you accept them at their level.

Note Writing

Notes are a delightful way to engage children in learning to write better. Write a little note and encourage them to write back, establishing back-and-forth communication between family members. Try writing notes to pack in the lunchbox or put in their backpack; slip it into their pocket or purse – whatever your child carries. Go high-tech by sending text messages to encourage each other to have a good day or send positive affirmations. Note writing could also be a daily communication method between parents and children. Kids may exchange notes or texts between younger or older siblings, cousins, aunts, or uncles.

Reminders

Teach kids to write reminders to themselves or others; otherwise, needed tasks may be overlooked. For example, they may need a reminder to take medication, submit an assignment, or ask a teacher about their scores. Help them establish the habit of writing it down. Adapt any ideas shared to fit family circumstances.

OTHER WRITING TASKS

Sample Prompt:

Write for 15 minutes continuously to produce multiple paragraphs. Choose one of the following topics:

Write about your favorite sport or activity for a sports magazine.

Write about your favorite artist (musician, music group, content creator, writer, etc.) for a music magazine.

Free choice:

Write about a topic of your choice to be published in a magazine of your choosing.

Writing has multiple purposes in our real lives. Students often feel disconnected from writing because assignments are usually just for the teacher, and the writing forms do not match pursuits beyond the classroom. Notice that the sample prompt assigns the writing to a specific person or group who will read or need the final product - real or imaginary. Authentic audiences solidify the need for writing.

Advice letters

Different issues arise in the community, and people have varying opinions. Secondary students will enjoy writing an advice letter to a local newspaper or a blog to offer advice about different situations. They could also advise younger children. My students write a letter to new middle schoolers when they enter 6th grade. They offer comfort after they have already experienced the same situation.

As we choose activities for kids, use the following questions as a guide:

What is an authentic structure for them to compose?

How might they mimic real-world writing or writing found in the wild world?

Mimicry

Try having kids mimic published writers. We know that too much formulaic writing sucks the joy out of composing, and we want kids to enjoy expressing themselves through writing. Use a line from a popular poem or story as a frame. Change the subject matter to creatively discuss your child's chosen topic. Allowing kids to write about what interests them is an important part of this activity. A full example of this activity is available in the REWRITE Workbook.

Leverage the Love for Argument

During adolescence, children begin to break away from adults in various ways. Debate with authority figures happens more frequently as they form their identities and their perspectives shift. Use one of their passionate arguments to prompt a writing challenge.

A parent's influence on a child's beliefs could wane during adolescence. They may begin to hold differing opinions. Forming personal views is part of growing up, and being an independent thinker is a hallmark of successful parenting. Academically challenge them by allowing them to wrestle with controversial issues and opposing viewpoints. Kids must be able to make their own decisions. Grant them the space to explore those ideas without shame.

Successful parents work themselves out of a job - not to be confused with working themselves out of a relationship.

SOCIAL MEDIA FOR BUSINESS PURPOSES

Social media is integral in academic and business networking. It is essential to have children use social media beyond forging friendships. Social media allows direct contact with people from various social and economic statuses. Kids may contact colleges and universities to follow up on reports and get expert opinions. Demonstrate multiple ways to use social media for business or academic purposes. How might tweens and teens use social media to conduct business? Think about ways to increase their opportunities for writing in the wild outside of the confines of school.

Here are a few more ideas:

- Writing reviews on Yelp and Google
- Writing movie reviews on Rotten Tomatoes or their own website
- Writing album or music reviews on popular websites or their own platform

Quick writes

Quick writes take five to ten minutes to record ideas in sentences and paragraphs. It does not closely attend to form and conventions. Quick writes may also be characterized as a rant under strong emotional circumstances.

WRITING AS CONFIDANT

The writing journal or diary can function as a confidant. Getting down complicated or emotional ideas and thoughts help kids to reflect on their life. Journals allow kids to untangle the ideas cluttering their minds. Give them a chance to write down that information. They will learn to unbraid that knot of emotions circulating and jumbling inside them. Use journaling to think through issues and "hormotions" (a mixture of hormones and emotions). It will be helpful as they grow up and reflect on life situations. You can model this for them.

I am not suggesting that you share all your secrets with children. Choose an issue that you feel comfortable sharing. For instance, there may be a conflict on the job. Maybe a colleague is doing something disingenuous or rude. Write about how to deal with it on a professional level. As children age, how they handle conflicts must shift to meet professional standards. "Going off" or cursing out colleagues on the job or at a place of business could be detrimental to their goals. We must coach our kids on handling tough situations; writing and reflection are one way. For kids, explain the issue, how to deal with it, and how to get it resolved. They will treasure the invaluable conversations about navigating professional friction as they encounter these kinds of experiences in the future.

Keeping a journal gives kids proof. They can lean on the track record told through their journals. When they go through a hard time again, they will already have the evidence that they got through rough times and can persevere again. In this way, the writing journal habituates writing daily and weekly. It teaches kids to build self-generated resources by creating a habit of turning to or confiding in their writing. With your support, they learn to work through feelings and emotions. When you are no longer there, they will possess a valuable coping strategy.

WORDS AS GIFTS

When kids create gifts with words and ideas that come from their minds, they are more genuine than when we buy store-bought gifts to give. Written gifts come from children - straight from their heart.

Poems, stories, and cards infused with creativity will invite them to fall in love with learning. Supply beautiful paper, make glitter, put designs, and have them give something to someone straight from their heart. Teaching them this skill will prove helpful.

Make sure the process is joyful. Do not let "thank you" letters become a forced obligation. Coach them in thinking about the joy the receiver gets from their show of appreciation. Remind them to think about bringing love into the ritual because we are motivating our child to be of service to loved ones - to reciprocate love.

CHAT G.P.T.

Chat G.P.T. and other forms of artificial intelligence can supplement our writing. Supplement by using A.I. to prompt ideas while allowing kids to develop the skill to articulate thoughts and emotions – their original thoughts and feelings that no one else can reproduce. Practice turning those thoughts into the written word will get our kids to the other side of their dreams. That experience will serve young learners for the rest of their lives.

Here are a few more ideas:

- A new law - explaining why it is unfair or fair
- Highlighting an injustice
- A petition to demand fair treatment or action
- Reflecting on conflicts
- Thinking through dilemmas
- Letter of appreciation to grandparents or a community member

Identify your son or daughter's areas of interest. What makes them tick right now? Understand that a child's interests change over time. As they move into new eras of their lives, update what they like and what they do not like. It may be increasingly more difficult to figure out. They may not be as expressive as they were when they were younger.

BORROWING FROM THEIR REAL-WORLD EXPERIENCES

If they play video games, have them talk and write about their video games. You can use comic books, graphic novels, or certain movies as topics.

Encourage children to ignite their passion by writing about topics they feel strongly about. If your child feels passionate about women's rights, then allow her to pen an argument on women's rights. To make a connection to real audiences, have them write to a magazine or a newspaper.

MOTIVATION THROUGH AGITATION

Have children read or watch a commentary that expresses the opposite opinion to one that they hold. They will often become angry or agitated enough to yell out counterarguments and rebuttals to the writer. It should be easy for them to produce a written response after hearing opposite opinions.

It may be slow at first. Kids may not feel compelled to engage, so families give up.

Too much time to choose can become a form of writing avoidance. Give teens and tweens one day to choose. Avoid allowing the choice to be the focus of the writing. Telling them the topic the day ahead will give them time to marinate on the subject matter.

Sometimes, children say they cannot make a choice. In those cases, provide three choices: two topics that you have chosen and one free choice. If they do not have their own ideas, they must choose one of the topics you have listed.

CHAPTER 4 REVIEW - R FOR REAL WORLD PURPOSES

In this chapter, we explored the significance of integrating writing into daily family activities. This approach serves multiple purposes: it encourages children to engage with writing, imparts essential life skills, and offers valuable insights into their writing abilities.

Align your child's interests with writing topics. This strategy is pivotal in sparking a young person's love for writing.

Proficiency in writing can significantly influence your child's life journey and contribute to your lasting legacy. Allowing them the freedom to express themselves without fear of judgment nurtures open lines of communication, especially during the tumultuous phases of hormonal changes and evolving social dynamics in adolescence.

I FOR INTENTIONAL PRACTICE

5

Intentional practice focuses on the skills and knowledge required to make progress. The previous chapters focused on cultivating a relationship with writing that includes choice, fun, and how to determine a child's writing level.

It is easy to stick with what is fun and engaging as we focus on writing development, but we have to apply pressure as well. Getting kids out of their comfort zone is essential to reaching adult-level writing proficiency.

Explain to kids when you are going to apply the pressure. Maintain enough variety for them to continue to feel successful so they will have enough gas in their tank to fuel them through the uphill battles.

You have been monitoring their writing, and you know their blindspots and what they need to work on. According to Readingrockets.org, "criteria can be tailored to a child's specific writing strengths and weaknesses, and can be modified as the child's abilities develop." Each writing task can measure different skills to target development in areas that match your child's needs.

GRADUAL RELEASE TEACHING MODEL

Take students through a process of modeling, practicing together, and independent practice. This will give them the on-ramp needed to gain the skill level necessary to try it on their own. Follow the Gradual Release Model for teaching.

Lessons begin "...with teachers demonstrating and modeling the learning for their own students – referred to as 'I do'." Here, the teacher is implementing approximately 90 percent of the 'heavy lifting' or work. (Archer & Hughes, 2011

As the lesson progresses, the students work with a partner or with the teacher to evenly distribute the work of figuring out or completing a task. During this portion, the students work in a group or with guided support. This part of the lesson can also be labeled as We Do.

Finally, children will demonstrate their knowledge or skills by working independently. This part of the lesson is also known as You Do. Even when you do not feel your child is ready for this stage, provide them with short independent practice to gather information about the particular area that still needs support.

ACHIEVING WRITING PROGRESS

Meet kids at their current level by providing an assessment, diagnostic, or anecdotal evidence (notes from a series of observations). The assessment results will provide a starting point. Remember, do not address all the writing issues simultaneously. Focus on one area that has a significant impact on their writing quality.

Set a Writing Goal

Create a S.M.A.R.T. goal (Specific, Measurable, Attainable, Relevant, Timebound). Assist teens and tweens in planning out the steps for completing their goal.

Use this three-step formula to cultivate growth:

Practice the skill: Plan to target this skill at least three times a week for about thirty days.

Write a task list for each practice session: Make time interval adjustments as needed. Instead of a new list daily, prioritizing a weekly task list may work better. Kids can check off each of the smaller tasks after completion.

Keep a reflection on progress: After practice sessions, record the glows (what is going well) and grows (what needs to improve).

Use supports as needed - Employ a variety of strategies for multiple opportunities to learn: instructional videos, spoken explanations, discussions (that help kids reflect on the concept and skills), demonstrations, and guided practice to support kids with internalizing the learning.

Collect student work - Keep writing materials together and date each paper or document to compare the writing before, during, and after the thirty days (or determined amount of time). In the future, this work shows evidence of growth over time.

Tips for Meeting Goals

Provide less supports each week, which will systematically move kids toward independence.

Consult The R.E.W.R.I.T.E. Workbook for goal-setting resources and activities.

TEAM ACTIVITIES

Collaborating with others can be highly beneficial in improving writing skills. One key advantage is the natural incentive to communicate. Thinking together creates a genuine reason to talk. Kids can leverage the recursive thinking, listening, writing, and speaking processes. Recursive means the cycle repeats, occurring over and over.

Writing is an extension of thinking, and working with others sparks creativity and strengthens thinking muscles because students will be processing the information continuously. Ultimately, kids will produce more robust completed written projects.

Collaborative writing activities and exercises

There are many ways to create a collaborative project or text. Joint writing activities and exercises are great tools for developing writing skills, promoting teamwork, and fostering creativity. Caregivers can write with their children, or a pair or group of kids can write together. Ideas for fun and engaging writing projects can include:

- Writing a story with alternating narrators. A narrative with two main characters may have portions from alternating viewpoints. Odd chapters can be in one character's voice and even chapters in the other character's voice. This activity allows each writer to bring their unique perspective to the story, creating a dynamic narrative that will keep readers engaged. Alternating chapters or sections between different characters can help each writer explore the story from different angles and develop their own voice and writing style.

- Write a two-voice poem to explore differing roles in a family, school, classroom, or team. Each writer on the team can contribute the same number of lines, allowing them to express their ideas while expanding on each other's work. The purpose of the poem could be to describe a day in the life. For example, an iteration of the poem can describe a mother's life while the other writer explores the life of another family member (father, son, daughter, or grandma). This activity is a great way to encourage teamwork and collaboration while developing language and communication skills.

- Create a story with multiple settings or worlds. The final product can feature one author's writing in one location, and the other author's work in an alternative universe. This activity allows each writer to create their unique setting or world, adding depth and complexity to the story. By working together, writers can create a rich account, providing a fun and engaging reading experience.

- Writing partners can present two sides of an issue in their editorial to promote critical thinking and argumentation skills. The team can construct solid arguments for both sides through discussion and reflection. By presenting both sides, writers can learn to consider multiple perspectives and develop thorough, evidence-based argumentative pieces. This activity advances writing skills essential for academic success.

KEYBOARDING SKILLS

Some adults think younger generations are digital natives who may not benefit from learning the basic typing skills of yesteryear. Research supports learning to type formally. It may hinder those who do not understand how to position their hands and type from the home row. Encourage kids to progress through a typing program that builds accuracy and speed to at least 40 words per minute. Fluent typing skills can enhance writing fluency by reducing the cognitive load associated with the physical act of typing. It will increase the speed of getting their work done and navigating the digital world more easily. Instead of leaving keyboarding skills to chance, ensure their comfort with typing.

Balance Typing and Writing

Be careful to maintain a balance between digital writing and pencil writing. On the opposite end of the spectrum, an over-reliance on technology will also disadvantage learners. Many children who learned to write during the pandemic did not practice writing with pencil and paper. Nurture both skills - typing and handwriting skills.

Formal handwriting

Children are developing writing skills using their style. Lack of standard letter formation causes legibility problems. Some students and families take offense to feedback on handwriting and sloppiness, but handwriting feedback is relevant when teaching conventions. For example, kids sometimes use capital letters in the middle of words.

Students are sometimes graded based on accuracy or how well they follow the rules for formal compositions. Assessments should inform instruction. If students need to learn the rules, devote lessons and practice to internalizing these rules.

When students write in all capital letters (caps) or compose whole passages in lowercase, have them correct the work to demonstrate their knowledge. Teach kids to evaluate situational appropriateness.

Writing assignments that require formal writing should be produced by following standards for forming letters, capitalization rules, grammar rules, and punctuation (mechanics).

Do not quash a student's style, but the audience, task, and purpose must align with the final product. When writing a note to a friend, informal writing is appropriate - as long as it is clear to the friend. Formal compositions may be the only acceptable form when completing a class assignment or writing to a notable person or group in authority. Each situation has varying expectations, so make them aware of the specifics. Practice meeting those requirements.

At this age, we not only want them to express themselves but to also prepare for the rigors of performing at a high level. We do not want people reading their work to be distracted by errors and missing their message. Maintain balance with kids on when to use informal and formal styles.

TESTING REQUIREMENTS

Invest time and energy into understanding any assessment your middle schooler needs to ace. There are various types of testing required for students to demonstrate their brilliance. For example, ninth graders may qualify for advanced placement (AP) courses that earn college credit. Writing proficiency can garner college credit, private school acceptance, scholarships, and more.

Analyze the test structure of any upcoming test several months in advance. Decide areas of the test that will reveal weaknesses, where children may be disadvantaged, and prepare for those disadvantages. Practice taking on the anticipated challenge so it is no longer an issue.

Sometimes a writing tool can throw kids off. Adults may not remember or even think of an issue with using an unfamiliar writing instrument, but kids miss having an eraser - especially if they have to take a high-stakes test with a pen (as some AP exams require). Make sure they develop comfortability with this writing tool. Confidence comes from employing the pen regularly. Designate a particular amount of time each week for pen and paper writing.

DEVELOPING STAMINA

Students may benefit from brief intervals of learning. For those who know you tend to get too entrenched, set a timer. At first, limit writing sessions to thirty minutes, but you may even have to build up to that time. If needed, limit sessions to ten minutes for the first week.

Be responsive to your child. If you want them to fall in love with writing (and they are not there yet), limit writing to short bursts. Give them a small amount of time, and make it engaging. Try to get them to a point that they want to continue, but stop anyway. Tell them, "You know what, we are out of time. Let's do more tomorrow." Keep them wanting more.

Taking advanced placement courses or the state examination requires stamina -- not just comfortability with writing. They must build up the ability to compose for about two hours, which develops over time. Allow for some endurance practice.

Many exclusive schools ask for an assessment, which includes a writing sample. Ask for the name of the test, the test structure, and the type of content assessed. Next, help them prepare. Make sure to target known weaknesses. Guide children in developing a growth mindset by giving them repeated attempts to get better at writing.

ERRORS TO AVOID

Balance informational texts with creative genres. Avoid scaffolding for too long. Even if you think they will not be successful, let them try completing a writing task on their own. It will give you information about their existing gaps and needs.

CHAPTER 5 REVIEW - I FOR INTENTIONAL PRACTICE

As children get older, more is required of them. It is important to know exactly what is required and support children in reaching these goals. Co-create writing goals with your child to be intentional in what and how you practice writing with them.

Collaborative activities, such as the two-voices poem, and alternating narrators challenge children to have fun and move beyond their present level of performance. By working with others, students can share ideas and brainstorm new concepts, which will spark their creativity. They can also engage in critical thinking by analyzing different perspectives and evaluating other arguments.

When selecting goals, consider upcoming testing requirements, keyboarding skills, handwriting, and writing stamina. Use the individual student's writing level, question stems from assessments, and the grade level requirements to inform the type of activities that will improve their proficiency.

T FOR WRITING TRAITS

6

Writing traits highlight specific areas of writing and provide the language and overarching concepts to discuss aspects of quality. Using these terms facilitates discussion in concrete terms to identify what makes a composition strong and areas that need to be strengthened. The acronym we use in the REWRITE Method is COW IS VP. This acronym orders the terms according to how the skills should be sequenced when teaching.

C is for conventions.

O is for organization.

W is for word choice.

I is for ideas.

S is for sentences - both structure and fluency.

V is for voice.

P is for publishing or the presentation.

Focusing on each of these writing traits will help produce writing that is objectively high quality. As students reach new levels of complexity in writing, it is normal for their work to be littered with mistakes. Trying and failing are part of the learning process. Some of these aspects of writing will be addressed during various stages of the writing process. For example, during the prewriting phase that may include making an outline as writers deal with organization. Later, writers may find that they need to also rearrange parts of the writing during the revision phase to improve organization.

C for Conventions

The C represents the conventions trait. This trait comes first because it is the easiest to address. This particular area of writing has to do with the correctness of the writing. There is an overlap between the stages of the writing process (Chapter 3, W for Writing Process). Remember, we use the acronym GUMSC to help us look for different aspects of correctness. Conventions measure how well the rules for grammar, usage, mechanics, spelling, and capitalization are followed. The acronym GUMSC focuses on the type of writing errors that need to be corrected. It teaches children how to check writing and internalize the steps. When a child takes a state test -- from grade 3 through 11 -- they should be able to read a prompt, analyze it, respond to it, as well as revise and edit errors on their own. Equipping children with an acronym representing areas to check before turning in work will give them confidence that they are submitting the highest quality writing possible.

O for Organization

O represents organization. Kids should be familiar with writing multiple paragraphs in middle school, which should have begun in upper elementary.

Organization involves logically sorting ideas, sentences, and paragraphs. First, choose a specific genre and match it with a specific type of thinking skill. For example, the thought process could involve comparing and contrasting or using cause and effect. Kids could be writing a problem-solution essay or composing a descriptive essay in which they are describing their topic. Another assignment could involve developing an argument and a counterargument to that central claim with evidence to support the opinion central to the paper.

Common Essay Types

- Comparison (Compare and Contrast)
- Causation (Cause and Effect)
- Problem-solving (Problem and Solution)
- Description (Descriptive - Top to Bottom)
- Argumentation

Teach children Freytag's Pyramid when writing narratives: beginning, middle, and end. The specifics of a story structure include exposition, inciting incident, rising action, climax, falling action, and resolution.

The workbook includes detailed diagrams related to various structures and how to present them to kids. You might be in the rare space where your children's teachers are already presenting these concepts to children, and the child does not need extra *this* year. If that is not the case, it is provided in the REWRITE Workbook. Make sure to use the language of the discipline when referring to the different types of writing structures and organization patterns.

W FOR WORD CHOICE

The word choice writing trait specifies the type of words used in a writing piece. We want our kids to identify words that work best for a particular topic or tone. Choosing the right vocabulary makes student writing shine. In middle school, state standards contain reading, writing, listening, and speaking standards that require sophisticated vocabulary in academic discussions and writing.

Informal versus Formal Language

To strengthen word choice, give children scenarios with varied communication purposes. For dialogue, allow them to choose between formal language and informal language. While hanging out with family and friends, informal language makes everyone comfortable. Informal language may overlap with a dialect -- or a language variation with marked differences from Standard American English. Depending on the writing task, informal language may be appropriate in precisely communicating what the character wants to say when writing dialogue between two characters. Other situations require formal speaking, such as interaction with an authority figure or getting vetted for a new job. There may even be judgment against people for not using the formal language or Standard American English. Make sure students are knowledgeable in dialect bias. We want to let them know that speaking differently is acceptable. They also need to be aware of what is situationally appropriate. They can choose according to the task, audience, and purpose of their writing.

Figurative Language

For middle school, it is vital to incorporate figurative language into student writing. Figures of speech, or figurative language, refers to wordplay or literary devices. These literary techniques can elevate writing from an elementary level to a middle school level. Figurative language receives emphasis in poetry, but wordplay appears in many forms of writing. In essays, comparisons are often made using similes and metaphors. Narratives often contain allusions to famous events, people, and biblical characters.

Common Figurative Language

- simile
- metaphor
- allusion
- idiom
- onomatopoeia
- pun

Specificity

Word choice also includes specificity. Challenge kids to get rid of – bury or banish – overused words, such as things, stuff, good, and nice. These are generic words.

Consider the sentences below:

- It tastes *good*.
- You did a *good* job.
- You are a *good* person.
- That skirt looks *good*.

For students to level up the quality of their writing, they should be aware that certain words lack specificity, and they do not enhance the meaning. Changing word choices to more specific terms happens in the revision phase. Instead of describing food as tasting good, challenge children to choose more vivid descriptions: spicy, tangy, sweet, salty, and other phrases to aid the reader's understanding of how the food tastes.

Banish Overused Words

The word "things" also represents a plethora, a whole spectrum of items. Encourage kids to trade in the word "things" for more fitting words: items, aspects, toys, and complaints.

For the word "stuff," challenge kids to make writing more specific. Trade out kindergarten-level words, such as "big," to polish up writing pieces to reflect grade-level quality. To choose from a range of words during revision, kids can look up words in an actual thesaurus or use a search engine for synonyms.

Sophisticated Words

Multisyllabic words can be three-syllable words and beyond. Challenge kids to use content area words for science and social studies. Let them know they are expected to use the words in context and for the appropriate situations.

I FOR IDEAS

Ideas refer to the details and information presented in a piece of writing. Adding sensory details is one way to revise for ideas.

Sensory Descriptions

Integrating the five senses can transform a scene into three-dimensional. The reader can hear, taste, smell, touch (feel), and see the objects through the descriptions. Children can use the five senses to describe and imagine worlds or to recreate any event or memory.

Provide the handout from the REWRITE Workbook with symbols representing each sense: noses, mouths, ears, eyes, and hands. Provide an exemplar text to analyze how sensory detail is used by the writer. Have children write-like the model (or exemplar text) to help them practice creating high level writing.

For example, a story or narrative may detail character and setting description. Narratives or stories focus on resolving a central conflict throughout character development, which includes dialogue, thoughts, actions, and what other characters say about another character.

When creating an informational piece, ideas consist of facts, statistics, opinions, and cited source material. Evidence can be connected through elaboration strategies that provide examples, define certain concepts, and detail other aspects of a topic. Ideas also include the main ideas and the details for informational genres. Ensure that the central idea is supported with evidence.

S FOR SENTENCE FLUENCY

Sentence fluency refers to the different structures of sentences in a text and how those sentences flow together. Children start with simple sentences when young because they can be as short as two or four words. For middle school, students need to move toward constructing paragraphs with varying sentence structures, including simple, compound, complex, and compound-complex sentences. As discussed in other chapters, achieve sentence fluency by revising to include various sentence starters.

Draft of a Paragraph without Sentence Variety

I like going to the store. I go to the store every day. I often like to meet new people in the store and talk to the store clerk.

Revised Paragraph for Sentence Variety

I like going to the store. Every day, my mother and I visit the store. We like talking to the store clerk and the other people visiting. In the future, I would like to own my own business.

In the first draft, the word "I" starts every sentence. Have students revise their writing to make the sentences flow smoothly or have better sentence fluency. Remember, there is a distinction between revision and editing. Revision is leveling up the writing by making it more sophisticated through improved sentence structure, word choice, and organization. Editing has to do with making the writing correct.

When revising for sentence fluency, add clauses to the beginning or invert the sentence for clarity or to improve the flow. We have workbook pages for practice inverting sentences and adding clauses to the beginning of sentences.

Another way to achieve sentence fluency is by having different lengths of sentences. It is acceptable to have a short sentence, but we only want some sentences to be short. Long sentences work for certain purposes, but it would be odd for all sentences to be compound-complex. Sentence fluency can involve combining sentences to eliminate choppiness.

V FOR VOICE

This element of writing is challenging to teach, and it is essential since it reveals the essence of a writer. It is their tone; it is their way of speaking, the way they use words.

When kids are trying to find their voice, they might use slang or certain phrasings that facilitate capturing their voice.

Think about voice as the personal style shown through how someone puts words together. Artificial intelligence (A.I.), like Chat G.P.T., does not have that voice or personality. Chat G.P.T. produces matter-of-fact, straight-to-the-point writing. It does not have a voice and style that shines through, compelling the reader to continue reading. The content is there, but the soul is gone. Make sure your child infuses individuality into their compositions.

Voice is one of the highest-leverage traits to develop. Some people naturally put their personality into their writing, but it is something we can all strive to achieve.

P FOR PRESENTATION

The P in COW IS VP refers to presentation. It is the final trait because it is the last aspect a writer needs to consider. Presentation refers to the overall appearance of a piece of writing. It focuses on how well the writing is visually presented, structured, and formatted.

There are several elements to consider in presentation:

1. Formatting: This refers to organizing text on the page, including paragraph breaks, headings, and subheadings. Proper formatting helps make the writing easier to read and understand.
2. Neatness and Legibility: The physical appearance of the writing can also impact its presentation. Neat and legible writing allows readers to understand the words and sentences easily.
3. Use of Fonts and Formatting Styles: Specific fonts and formatting styles may be required or preferred depending on the context.

Following the teacher's guidelines or the writing prompt can contribute to a polished and formal presentation.

4. Graphics and images: Choose graphics, charts, and other images (or pictures) that can enhance the understanding of the topic. If the writing has statistics and trends, a chart or graphic can be included to illustrate the information. If it is a narrative, pictures or drawings of the characters and setting may be included.

Overall, presentation can make writing look professional, well-structured, and easy to read. By paying attention to presentation, parents can help their children create final drafts that are visually appealing and effectively communicate their ideas.

CHAPTER 6 REVIEW T FOR TRAITS

Chapter 6 is all about diving into the fundamental aspects of writing that help us recognize what makes great writing and where improvements can be made. Adapt tools and strategies to your child's needs. As you get more involved in writing support, you will become an expert on your child's needs.

The acronym C.O.W. I.S. V.P. represents the writing traits in the sequence recommended for teaching: conventions, organization, word choice, ideas, sentences, voice, and presentation. Each of these traits is like a puzzle piece that contributes to the bigger picture of excellent writing.

Conventions cover the rules and norms that govern writing. Organization focuses on how ideas are arranged. Word choice highlights the significance of selecting just the right words to convey meaning effectively. Ideas are the core substance of any written work. Sentence structure and sentence fluency allow the writing to flow smoothly and clearly. Voice refers to the unique personality injected into writing. Presentation details the look and the layout when a piece of writing is shared with an audience.

By teaching the writing traits, we encourage creative exploration. IIt gives them permission to embrace quality in their writing endeavors. These are the traits that serve as guideposts, giving us a common language to discuss and understand the quality of writing.

E FOR ENCOURAGING CREATIVITY

7

Many educators perceive writing as rigid, primarily focusing on rule-following and corrections. However, the truth is that writing development flourishes when infused with creativity and the freedom of choice. As Readingrockets.org aptly points out, writing can be a powerful tool for developing critical thinking skills, which are increasingly encouraged in various facets of a student's education. The REWRITE Method provides a framework for nurturing thoughtful, innovative young writers—not merely obedient students who conform to predefined templates.

Here are common statements and questions from students who have been indoctrinated in a rigid writing stance:

- Aren't paragraphs 4 sentences?
- Paragraphs are supposed to be 6 sentences, right?
- We are only doing 5 paragraphs, right?
- How do I start?

Teaching writing is messy, especially in a class with dozens of children who are all on different stages of the process with differing needs.

In their well-intentioned support, teachers provide a template for the opening sentence of the first paragraph and sentence frames for the second paragraph, and it continues to the conclusion of the essay. While this type of support may be helpful for a small group of students, it stifles the majority of learners bursting with ideas and innovation. Attempts to streamline writing instruction by enforcing uniformity leads to a robotic style of writing, far from the essence of authentic expression. It is not real writing; it is writing by numbers.

When students are hand-held through every stage of the writing process, this produces a proliferation of nearly identical essays. Critical thinking often takes a backseat as students tend to produce what their teacher instructs them to write in the manner prescribed by the teacher, adhering to the style the teacher dictates for expressing ideas.

In this environment, many children fail to associate creativity with writing. They find themselves stuck, unsure of how to begin, and often paralyzed by the fear of making mistakes. When it comes to writing, they have developed a deep-seated belief that they are bound to get it wrong. Creative expression and individual opinions have been corrected out of them.

WARNING - GET UNSTUCK FROM THE FIVE-PARAGRAPH ESSAY

Many secondary teachers get stuck in the five-paragraph essay without teaching other structures involving organization and thinking skills. The five-paragraph structure is a third through twelfth-grade writing format. The five-paragraph essay does not exist in college. That is why parents and teachers should use authentic writing pieces easily found worldwide - newspapers, magazines, blogs, newsletters, novels, short stories, and other written works.

Instead of a five-paragraph essay, have kids write an editorial or design and write the content for a web page. As a guide, students may fashion it after an existing website that discusses dinosaurs. Kids can riff off the model. Ask students questions in the planning phase.

Example questions might be:

- How might your page be structured like this?
- How would you make your page different?

Find authentic writing examples that exist in the wild. Look for real-world purposes and widely published genres for student writing assignments. Most published essays do not follow a five-paragraph essay format. The five-paragraph essay stunts student progress regarding high-stakes testing, college application essays, and cover letters.

It is time to grant children creative license when they write. Drawing from my experience as an English Language Arts Advisor for numerous schools, I have observed secondary writing narrow into a singular focus on the dreaded five-paragraph essay. Children should have the choice to write poems, blogs, articles, rants, and other genres to respond to their world, written texts, and visual texts.

The R.E.W.R.I.T.E. Method adheres to researched best practices crafted by experienced classroom educators. This structured instruction embraces creativity and acknowledges the value of making mistakes as integral to the writing development process. At its core, it promotes writing as an enjoyable and liberating experience. Permitting young writers to express themselves in multiple styles and embrace learning from their errors to pave the way for true growth in writing.

ENCOURAGE

You may be reading this book because your child's writing is atrocious. While that may be true, you must find some aspect of your child's writing to compliment. It could be as simple as handwriting. To entice your child to love writing and learn how to write better, they must experience success. Constructive feedback builds on what they already do well - even if it is just forming letters neatly (Chapter 2 - E for Effective Feedback).

The goal is to cultivate your child's genius and increase motivation. Reward their work with verbal praise about their areas of improvement. Avoid empty compliments like "good job". Point out the particular aspects of their writing that are strong. Collaboratively set goals with your child. Agree on rewards, such as an afternoon at the movies, an ice cream extravaganza, or a bike-riding adventure. Of course, the reward should be something valuable to your child. As children change, so do their interests. Be sure to get their input about the incentives that make them excited.

BE POSITIVE

Writing is a constant in our daily lives. Watch your words and your body language when it comes to writing. Frame written tasks in a positive way when you have a writing task.

Try saying:
- I have the opportunity
- I get to ...

Remember that if you treat writing like a gift, your child will welcome the challenge.

Avoid negative phrases:

- I have to ...
- I've got to ...

AVOID DISCOURAGEMENT

Some children do not like writing. It may surprise you that attitudes against composition have been perpetuated in our homes – maybe even by you. Think about what you say and do when it is time to write.

Remember that if you treat writing like a burden, it will transfer to your child. In my family, I have heard many negative messages:

- I am not writing all of that.
- I do not know why there is so much writing; I am not reading all that.
- Your writing is sloppy. I cannot even read it.

Writing Punishments

Many parents employ the ultimate way to turn a child against writing by making writing a negative consequence.

- You cannot leave this room until you write an apology.
- Write "I will not disobey" 500 times.

Those who lack writing skills will be limited in their academic and career pursuits. Ineffective writing will result in unrealized dreams and unfulfilled lives.

POSSIBILITIES

People who have mastered manipulation of the written word can get almost anything they want. Many high-paying jobs require passing a written test, and well-crafted essays earn scholarships, admission into college, and garner dream job offers.

Think about hit writers: playwrights, bloggers, novelists, and children's authors. Many have earned millions of dollars, and they secure lucrative deals because of their imagination and insight.

Help from Famous Creatives

Use literature from notable writers as mentor texts - a published piece of writing used as a model for the final product. The style and structure of the original author's writing can guide the child's writing. Creativity comes from crafting a message about a different topic. Invite children to think about how they can adapt the original to create their finished piece.

The REWRITE Method minimizes formulaic essay writing. Start by finding examples in the wild world. Observe spoken word poets and analyze a transcript of their performed poems. Consult a book of poetry and songs – by both rappers and singers. Study song lyrics and have your tween read, analyze, and mimic their style for practice. Book reviews can replace book reports. Instead of research reports, children can create investigative reports like the ones found in newspapers and magazines.

Avoid squeezing the joy out of writing; allow kids to be creative when they write at home. Think about all the ways you could be creative. The REWRITE Workbook details creative writing exercises that simultaneously build skills and motivate young people to write.

Have children try out new strategies and figurative language. For example, have them practice varying sentence lengths. Pull some great sentences from those magical lyricists, writers, rappers, or spoken word artists. Have them try to write like them by using a sentence frame that keeps the essential part of a stand-out sentence. Demonstrate how they can do something different – turn that phrase around and make it their own.

Challenging Topics

Please do not censor our middle schoolers on what they write. They will write about some issues in ways that are no longer cute or pretty. Give adolescents the space to process as they find the essence of their writing voice. If you do not, someone else will. That someone else may not be a source of reliable information or good advice. As caregivers, we want our homes to be where they can write whatever they want without judgment and punishment for their thoughts.

Choose an Audience

An audience shapes a written message. If the audience is kindergarteners or middle schoolers, the word choice will be very different. On the other hand, writing for parents will have another set of differences. Children should have an authentic audience when they are writing. Give them a task that relates to real-world activities. The audience can be one kid looking at herself in the mirror or a performance from supportive family members.

OTHER METHODS

Other techniques that stimulate imagination and creativity can come from remixing well-known stories. Reimagine the story from another character's point of view. For example, Goldilocks and Three Bears have already published books written from Mother Bear's, the baby bear's, or Papa Bear's perspective. That creates a whole new story and unleashes their creativity, giving them the creative license to try something new.

Students may write the sequel to Goldilocks. How do the three bears react to Goldilocks' thievery? Do they go to Goldilocks' home to report her behavior to her parents? Will Goldilocks repair her damage by volunteering and replacing items in the Bear family's home? How do the families continue to interact after this incident?

Another iteration of this challenge could be for teens to write from the perspective of characters in another story, such as Mufaro's Beautiful Daughters. This time, challenge them to switch the tone for each scene. Explore how characters would manifest curiosity, fear, sadness, and anger. Help your child think through probing questions. How would their assigned emotion change the actions made during different scenes? Discuss how the character would act and the dialogue. Just responding with laughter, interest, and questions could be a great way to cultivate creativity to help them fall in love with writing.

Social Media

Social media can support writing development. While many people use social media for social purposes, it is also valuable in growing businesses and collaborating in academic circles. Teach your child how to create social media posts for academic purposes.

Presentations

Parents could also create gifts for kids or other family members to commemorate mothers, fathers, and others. In turn, kids can use the parents' original written gift to create their version for the same family member or someone new. Plan to perform or give these written gifts during family events or community gatherings. Juneteenth festivities, Independence Day celebrations, and family reunions lend themselves to presentations by youth. Have children perform writing assignments for an authentic audience in front of actual people to build speaking skills and confidence.

ERRORS TO AVOID

Avoid spending over an hour on heavy-lifting academics. Provide breaks and a variety of activities to keep them engaged and stimulated.

Do not underestimate your power. Parents and caregivers can support youngsters in fortifying learning skills year after year. Families have more influence than individual teachers, who usually only work with kids for one nine-month school year.

Avoid writing for school-only purposes. Although you may verbally stress the importance of writing, kids absorb actions better than spoken words. Make writing part of your family's daily life to ensure your child understands its importance through actions.

CHAPTER 7 REVIEW E FOR ENCOURAGING CREATIVITY

Writing instruction in many schools tends to be overly prescriptive.

This chapter explores ways to infuse creativity into writing: motivation, positivity, linking writing proficiency to opportunities, and ceasing discouraging actions.

Many teachers and parents neglect the aspect of motivation when planning writing lessons. Allow students to take ownership for constructing their writing capacity by giving them a choice of writing tasks or topics. As parents and teachers, we must project positivity when discussing our personal writing and how we frame writing setbacks. Children pick up on our negativity toward writing and will internalize a deficit mindset in relation to writing. Remind children how writing proficiency affords many opportunities.

As we guide young writers, we must also avoid discouraging habits: writing punishments, focusing on one type of writing, and censoring topics. Collaborate with students consistently, so they will be motivated and inspired to hone their personal writing prowess.

ELEMENTARY TO MIDDLE SCHOOL WRITING STANDARDS

The Common Core State Standards for Writing challenge students to produce a specific amount (length of time and number of words), genres, the level of writing (sentence types, organization, and features), and the differences between grade levels.

Depending on your child's school or state of residence, they may or may not be using Common Core State Standards. The CCSS direct learning requirements in about 17 states at the time of this printing. They describe the information students should learn in a particular grade level. Be sure to refer to your specific state's guidelines when you are preparing your children for success on their state test, an assessment your child needs to pass to move on to the next level or gain entrance into the school of their choice. We know middle schools, high schools, and even dual enrollment programs have different assessments, standards, and benchmarks.

This chapter details the requirements between 5th and 6th grade. While it is essential to know your child's level of performance, you should also understand expectations according to specific grade levels. These learning standards provide the parameters of state tests, grades, placement exams, private school entrance exams, and other assessments.

Familiarizing yourself with the learning standards helps you know what your child needs and their expected level of performance. Standards provide a guideline for purposeful practice that builds toward the end goal or target learning goal. If your child is ready, they can move beyond the standard as long as you are sure they have mastered the basics.

The Common Core State Standards (CCSS) for writing from 5th (elementary) to 6th grade (middle school) contain three standards for each broad writing form produced in middle school.

Standard 1 - Argument writing

Standard 2 - Informative or Explanatory writing

Standard 3 - Narrative writing

Note that standards reflect the end-of-year learning outcomes. These goals are very similar to grade 5 standards; however, there are differences.

For argument (standard 1), students support an opinion (referred to as a *claim* in the standard's wording).

For informational or explanatory writing (standard 2), kids explain complicated ideas and information clearly and correctly (accurately).

Kids compose actual or imagined events for narrative compositions (standard 3).

The requirements include more complex and higher-level skills than the 5th grade standards.

When our children have holes in their understanding, we can look to those lower standards to see the delineated prerequisite skills. We can also notice skills not explicitly described. It may be beneficial to return to lower levels to shore up those early-grade skills to ensure they are ready for more advanced requirements for each preceding grade level.

Analysis of the writing standards between fifth and sixth grade details what aspects of writing need to level up from elementary and the expectations required of our middle schoolers.

The CCSS has been adopted by seventeen states (at the time of this printing). Each state's CCSS contains some variations because their governing bodies decided to add a couple of extra standards. Consult your specific state website for the CCSS. Mandated tests may feature these skills and affect your child's college admissions.

We will focus on writing, but there is a lot of overlap between reading, writing, listening, and speaking. There is also a language domain of the standards for grammar and usage skills, which overlap with the writing standards.

Text Types and Purposes

WRITING STANDARD 1 OPINION AND ARGUMENT WRITING

When writing an argument, valid reasoning explains the viewpoint or opinion. The standard also calls for relevant and sufficient evidence. The evidence must relate to the topic and the idea at the center of the argument. Sufficient means that there needs to be enough supporting information, and it needs to be credible (believable) and reliable.

5.1 opinion	6.1 argument
Write opinion pieces on topics or texts, supporting a point of view with reasons and information.	Write arguments to support claims with clear reasons and relevant evidence.

5th grade writing standard 1 is labeled Opinion. In sixth grade, writing standard 1 is labeled Argument. When developing an argument, claims refer to opinion. 6th graders need to base their argument on fact, while fifth graders only need to provide a clear opinion with reasons. 6th graders must find statistics, facts, and data to support their views. There is a requirement to base their opinion on evidence. This aligns with the need to cite sources that support their viewpoint, which correlates with reading standards.

Writing 5.1A	Writing 6.1A
Introduce a topic or text clearly, state an opinion, and create an organizational structure in which ideas are logically grouped to support the writer's purpose.	Introduce claims and organize the reasons and evidence clearly.

The 6th grade standard uses fewer words because of an implication of the lower level skills. For fifth grade, the organizational structure should logically group ideas. The verbiage in 6th grade states to "organize the reasons and evidence clearly." Infer the requirement for the unstated skills (logically grouping ideas), which implies that logical grouping should be mastered in the 5th grade.

Writing 5.1B	Writing 6.1B
Provide logically ordered reasons that are supported by facts and details.	Support claims with clear reasons and relevant evidence, using credible sources and demonstrating an understanding of the topic or text.

Writing 5.1B is less of a heavy lift because 5th graders only need to "logically order reasons" with "facts and details." In 6th grade, students need to also determine if a text is a credible source, adding another layer of complexity. We must teach children how to determine if a source is reliable. One method involves analyzing for accountability. Lack of accountability refers to someone who publishes in isolation without fearing job loss, damaging their reputation, or losing advertising revenue.

Ask the following questions:

Will the audience be able to sue and recover damages?

Is the author or creator an established professional or a business representative with a trusted reputation?

Writing 5.1C	Writing 6.1C
Link opinion and reasons using words, phrases, and clauses (e.g., consequently, specifically).	Use words, phrases, and clauses to clarify the relationships among claims and reasons.

6th graders need to do more than just link opinions and reasons. They need to clarify the relationship. When presenting an opposing idea, they need to note that it is a comparison or cause and effect. They need to describe the relationship among claims and reasons.

Writing 6.1D

Establish and maintain a formal style.

Writing 6.1 D is a concise standard. There is not a similar requirement for 5th grade. Lessons teaching formal style include eliminating contractions, spellings, and conventions used in text messages (i, u, ur, lmk), and other abbreviations.

Fixing Text Message Spellings and Conventions

- Ur changed to your or you are
- I'm changed to I am

Other Abbreviations

- ASAP = as soon as possible or immediately
- NBD = no big deal
- Addy = address
- Btw = by the way

The pronoun I

Some teachers require children to take the pronoun "I" out of their work to maintain a formal style. That requirement is becoming less common, but make this decision based on the audience and purpose of the writing task.

Revising from informal to formal style also includes eliminating shortened forms of phrases.

Commonly shortened phrases

- gonna (going to)
- wanna (want to)

List of Contractions

- I've changed to I have
- We're changed to we are
- Ain't changed to is not

Writing 5.1D	Writing 6.1E
Provide a concluding statement or section related to the opinion presented.	Provide a concluding statement or section that follows from the argument presented.

For the fifth grade, W 5.1D and W 6.1E are very similar. The conclusion paragraph asks for a few details in either standard. The conclusion can be as brief as one sentence. The REWRITE Workbook provides a few examples. Students can be taught to create a conclusion section, but this part of the essay can be a few sentences in this stage of the learning progression.

WRITING STANDARD 2 - INFORMATIVE/EXPLANATORY TEXTS

Explanatory or informative writing needs to have organization and include an analysis of content. Analysis involves breaking down the information into smaller chunks to demonstrate an understanding of the information presented.

W 5.2 Informative/explanatory texts	W 6.2 Informative/explanatory texts
Write informative/explanatory texts to examine a topic and convey ideas and information.	Write informative/explanatory texts to examine a topic and convey ideas, concepts, and information through the selection, organization, and analysis of relevant content.

Notice the increase in verbiage between the fifth and sixth grade standards. The additional words give added demands and move from two categories of content (ideas and information) to measuring three categories (ideas, concepts, and information). The standard further explains how to do this: "through the selection, organization, and analysis of relevant content." So, the content needs to be related to the topic. Children need to know how to select or choose sources (texts and other media), organize the sources (place the content in the appropriate part of their essay), and analyze (break down the ideas, concepts, and information) for the audience to gain a clear understanding.

W 5.2A	W 6.2A
Introduce a topic clearly, provide a general observation and focus, and group related information logically; include formatting (e.g., headings), illustrations, and multimedia when useful to aiding comprehension.	Introduce a topic; organize ideas, concepts, and information, using strategies such as definition, classification, comparison /contrast, and cause /effect; include formatting (e.g., headings), graphics, (e.g., charts, tables), and multimedia when useful to aiding comprehension.

Fifth and sixth grades are similar, but they use different strategies to present information. The 5th grade does not mention graphics, but the 6th grade requires both graphics and charts. Both levels require the graphics to be useful in aiding comprehension. Sometimes kids just add graphics because it is pretty. Help them to recognize how graphics support the audience's understanding of what is being presented.

W 5.2B	W. 6.2B
Develop the topic with facts, definitions, concrete details, quotations, or other information and examples related to the topic.	Develop the topic with relevant facts, definitions, concrete details, quotations, or other information and examples.

There are only a few differences between these two standards. For fifth grade, the examples need to be related to the topic. In sixth grade, the examples also need to be relevant, which refers to meaningful connections to the topic.

W 5.2C	W 6.2C
Link ideas within and across categories of information using words, phrases, and clauses (e.g., in contrast, especially).	Use appropriate transitions to clarify the relationships among ideas and concepts.

Writing 5.2C and 6.2C correlate with Writing 6.1C that requires students to clarify relationships. Students are challenged to learn how to write essays and clarify the relationships through transitions. In fifth grade, they only need to link the ideas using phrases and clauses. For sixth grade, the relationships need to be clarified. The relationships can be defined as similar, in opposition, in time-order, or indicate cause and effect.

W 5.2D	W 6.2D
Use precise language and domain-specific vocabulary to inform about or explain the topic.	Use precise language and domain-specific vocabulary to inform about or explain the topic.

These are identical standards. The same skill is being taught in sixth and fifth grades. Word choice needs to be developed for at least a couple of years. When officials authored the standards, they used developmental appropriateness. As a parent, determine how long your child needs to develop or thoroughly learn a skill.

Writing 6.2E
Establish and maintain a formal style.

This standard echoes Writing Standard 6.1E. Fifth graders learn about formal style, but sixth graders have a new requirement to write formally in various genres.

Writing 5.2E*	W 6.2F
Provide a concluding statement or section related to the information or explanation presented.	Provide a concluding statement or section that follows from the information or explanation presented.

W5.2E and W6.2F are similar. The standards indicate students may not master or fully grasp this skill in 5th grade, so they will continue to work on it in 6th grade. Conclusions are essential paragraphs in essays.

WRITING STANDARD 3 - NARRATIVES

Narratives are stories that center around solving a conflict. Students must learn how to craft a series of events to entertain audiences. Narratives come in many media forms: plays, novels, short stories, and movies. In secondary schools, narratives and other creative writing are often frowned upon because of the focus on standardized testing that favors informational and argumentative genres.

W 5.3	W 6.3
Write narratives to develop real or imagined experiences or events using effective techniques, descriptive details, and clear event sequences	Write narratives to develop real or imagined experiences or events using effective technique, relevant descriptive details, and well-structured event sequences.

Effective Techniques

To create an engaging narrative, it is important to use narrative techniques to draw in the audience. Dialogue and pacing are two different techniques used in stories.

Descriptive Details

Sensory details describe a scene using some or all of the five senses. Narratives also use figurative language or literary devices such as simile, metaphor, onomatopoeia, analogy, and alliteration to describe emotions, actions, and scenes.

Well-structured event sequences

The standard only requires clear event sequences for fifth grade. For my sixth graders, I teach the plot structure diagram – which is also known as Freytag's Pyramid – that outlines different parts of the narrative to make it flow well and build the reader's anticipation. A well-structured event sequence includes exposition, inciting incident, rising action, climax, falling action, and resolution. More information about Freytag's Pyramid and narrative structure is found in the REWRITE Workbook.

The language for fifth grade differs according to the type of details. There needs to be relevant descriptive details. Suppose children write five pages to describe a scene in a story. In that case, those details need to be related to solving the conflict. The details may also reveal something within a character that is related to the overall narrative, such as uncovering motivations.

Writing 5.3A	Writing 6.3A
Orient the reader by establishing a situation and introducing a narrator and/or characters; organize an event sequence that unfolds naturally.	Engage and orient the reader by establishing a context and introducing a narrator and/or characters; organize an event sequence that unfolds naturally and logically.

6th graders have additional requirements, such as creating event sequences that unfold naturally as well as logically. They not only need to orient the reader, but also engage the reader by establishing a context. In fifth grade, writers only need a situation. Describing a context for the narrative involves explaining what is happening in the world – whatever world the child is building in the narrative. The setting or world could be real or imagined. For example, it may be set in the future, in the year 2046. The context may be that it is the night of the election when the first robot is elected president of the United States.

Writing 5.3B	Writing 6.3B
Use narrative techniques such as dialogue, description, and pacing to develop experiences and events or show the responses of characters to situations.	Use narrative techniques, such as dialogue, pacing, and description, to develop experiences, events, and/or characters.

The key difference is developing experiences and events instead of just showing responses to situations. That part is implied in the 6th grade instead of explicitly detailed.

When constructing experiences, it is important to note that setting description includes both time and place. Although it is taught in fifth grade, we want to make sure to remind middle schoolers. A narrative that takes place in Los Angeles, California in 1966 will be very different from a story set in Los Angeles in 2046.

W 5.3C	W.6.3C
Use a variety of transitional words, phrases, and clauses to manage the sequence of events.	Use a variety of transition words, phrases, and clauses to convey sequence and signal shifts from one time frame or setting to another.

For standard 5.3 C and 6.3 C, there is a focus on transitional words. 6th grade adds depth by requiring a shift from one time frame or setting to another. The setting could also specify the season. Los Angeles in January 1966 and June 1966 are also different settings as well. Within the context of setting, time can mean time of day, time of year (season), or calendar year.

W 5.3D	W 6.3D
Use concrete words, phrases, and sensory details to convey experiences and events precisely.	Use precise words, phrases, relevant descriptive details, and sensory language to convey experiences and events.

To convey experiences and events, consider using emotions. What emotions might the characters have? Sensory language refers to the five senses like in the fifth grade. In the sixth grade, we also want the emotion to be named and explained.

W 5.3E	W 6.3E
Provide a conclusion that follows from the narrated experiences or events.	Provide a conclusion that follows from the narrated experiences or events.

In a narrative, this standard calls for the "happily ever after" part. In Freytag's Pyramid this is the resolution. The writer answers the question - What happens from then on in the characters' future? For example, a story may have something like "the wolf never bothered the pigs again." It is a conclusion that explains what happens after the story ends.

WRITING STANDARDS 4 - 6: PRODUCTION AND DISTRIBUTION OF WRITING

WRITING STANDARD 4 - CLEAR AND COHERENT WRITING

These writing standards are general and do not apply to a specific genre. Standard four focuses on the production and distribution of writing, emphasizing the need for clear and coherent written expression.

W 5.4	W 6.4
Produce clear and coherent writing in which the development and organization are appropriate to the task, purpose, and audience.	Produce clear and coherent writing in which the development, organization, and style are appropriate to the task, purpose, and audience.

Students must match the task, purpose, and audience. For example, appropriate organization and language may be informal, such as slang used by their peers. No matter the genre, the writing should be clear and appropriate to the task and audience.

The difference between 5th and 6th grade: style. When considering style, think about developing a voice using words and phrases that sound like your child. We can listen to what they say and do (how quickly or slowly they speak) when they are talking to give them some style hints. They may also decide to infuse some creativity or give a character an accent that they do not use in their own speaking. Style can also include terms and phrases. Overall, speaking style and word choice can give us a clue about how to develop style.

WRITING STANDARD 5 - THE WRITING PROCESS

Standard five addresses the development and strengthening of writing. Students engage in the various stages of the writing process to develop a complete writing task. During planning and prewriting, they should carefully consider their ideas and structure. During revision, they improve the quality of their writing. During editing, they should correct any errors. After receiving feedback, they should rewrite their work to try new styles and refine their ideas.

W 5.5	W 6.5
With guidance and support from peers and adults, develop and strengthen writing as needed by planning, revising, editing, rewriting, or trying a new approach. (Editing for conventions should demonstrate command of Language standards 1-3 up to and including grade 5 here.)	With some guidance and support from peers and adults, develop and strengthen writing as needed by planning, revising, editing, rewriting, or trying a new approach. (Editing for conventions should demonstrate command of Language standards 1-3 up to and including grade 6 here.)

The standards differ concerning the amount of support. In 5th grade, students get full guidance and support, while 6th graders get less (some guidance). This signals that students should not be guided step-by-step through the writing process. Instead, prompt secondary students to employ the acronyms and other strategies practiced with teachers (parents) and peers. Below, a set of guiding questions are provided. Note that another area of the standards inform the editing guidelines. The cumulative Language standards – referring to all the grades before and including the current grade – detail the exact skills that students should know when it comes to the type of corrections or grammar, usage, mechanics, spelling, and capitalization rules that need to be followed.

Questions to Guide Students Through the Writing Process:

- How will you gather ideas before writing sentences and paragraphs?
- What are the moves that need to be made when it is time to revise?
- At what stage of the process will they try a new beginning, change the ending, or rearrange details?
- What acronym can be used that names what needs to be edited?

WRITING STANDARD 6 - WRITING USING TECHNOLOGY

Standard six emphasizes the use of technology. Students utilize technology for writing tasks, such as typing their work and exploring different formats and platforms for publishing. They are also encouraged to interact and collaborate with others, sharing and discussing their writing.

W 5.6	W 6.6
With some guidance and support from adults, use technology, including the Internet, to produce and publish writing as well as to interact and collaborate with others; demonstrate sufficient command of keyboarding skills to type a minimum of two pages in a single sitting	Use technology, including the Internet, to produce and publish writing as well as to interact and collaborate with others; demonstrate sufficient command of keyboarding skills to type a minimum of three pages in a single sitting.

For W 5.6., students are not expected to need a lot of help. W 6.6 states that sixth graders use technology, implying that they are expected to do this on their own. This is clear when we compare the grade 5 standard, that includes an additional phrase that indicates that some guidance is needed.

Produce Writing Using Technology

Producing writing using technology refers to typing their work inside Microsoft Word, Google Docs, or another word processing program. Using the spell check, grammar check, and other review resources includes producing writing using technology. They may also embed images, format for double spacing, use various fonts, colors, and other features to enhance their work.

Publish Using Technology

Publishing involves making the writing public and presenting it for an audience. There are many possibilities: printing the completed text to post it on a board, exhibiting it on a class website, emailing it to the intended audience, making it public on a blog, posting it on a social media platform, and recording a reading of the work (and posting that online). Your child can choose to publish their work in three different ways.

Interact and Collaborate

Interacting using technology could be having online discussions. Students can provide comment-only or suggestions access to a Google doc so that classmates can add comments and suggestions to a peer's published work or work-in-progress. This could be part of the peer review, editing process, or publishing celebration.

Collaboration can also take many forms. For example, students can co-write a report, essay, or narrative by sharing an editable Google Doc, having different members of the group produce different parts of a report (partner 1 - labeled images and 2 paragraphs, partner 2 - Works Cited and 2 paragraphs).

Amount of Writing

Another key difference is the amount of writing. 5th graders should be able to type a minimum of two pages in a single sitting. This standard is measurable. Do we have two pages? Get down to the nitty gritty with this: 12-point font, double-spaced pages. Do not allow children to use 16-point font and get credit for two pages. Think in terms of the volume that they need to be writing.

5th graders need to compose extra pages: three pages in a single sitting. We need to make sure that children know how much they should be writing. They should work toward building writing stamina, and use three pages as a criteria when measuring their progress towards meeting the standard.

The state assessment is not timed, but it is normal for a proficient writer to take about two hours (on average) to complete the long-form writing assessment or performance task. The performance task involves reading at least three texts and writing several paragraphs to respond to a prompt that integrates information from the texts. Advanced Placement examinations, which are administered nationwide, also require on-demand writing.

This is the last grade level with specific page requirements from CCSS. I assume the volume of writing does not increase in page length until the 12th grade. Instead, the quality scales up from here in terms of depth and complexity. Very few inner-city high schools – let alone middle schools – ask their students to write three pages (which is a requirement since 6th grade). Yet colleges and universities regularly assign five-page reports and beyond. When parents know standards in-depth, we can help support students as they transition into adulthood and meet the demands of college and careers.

WRITING STANDARDS 7 - 9: RESEARCH

The research standards covered under standards seven, eight, and nine, focus on research projects and gathering relevant information. Students use print and digital sources and evaluate the credibility of all researched documents. They should integrate information effectively and avoid plagiarism. Standard nine highlights the importance of drawing evidence from literary and informational texts to support analysis, reflection, and research.

WRITING STANDARD 7 - RESEARCH PROJECTS

W 5.7	W 6.7
Conduct short research projects that use several sources to build knowledge through the investigation of different aspects of a topic.	Conduct short research projects to answer a question, drawing on several sources and refocusing the inquiry when appropriate.

For W 5.7, fifth graders read several texts and media sources to learn about different categories of information about a topic. Sixth graders begin with a question, indicating that there is another layer of responsibility than required in 5th grade. Middle schoolers start with a question and conduct research. Next, learners reflect on the question they asked at the beginning and refocus it. Kids may want to know more about why dinosaurs are extinct instead of knowing about the different types of dinosaurs. They should reach a more focused inquiry or question to research. This standard gets them to a deeper level of understanding. Sometimes they get lost in what they have chosen. Helping them refocus their questions will flex their critical thinking.

WRITING STANDARD 8 - INTEGRATING SOURCES

W 5.8	W 6.8
Recall relevant information from experiences or gather relevant information from print and digital sources; summarize or paraphrase information in notes and finished work, and provide a list of sources.	Gather relevant information from multiple print and digital sources; assess the credibility of each source; and quote or paraphrase the data and conclusions of others while avoiding plagiarism and providing basic bibliographic information for sources.

Fifth graders need to recall relevant information. This is a low-level thinking skill that involves remembering. For 6th grade, they gather relevant information from multiple print and digital sources.

Assessing the Credibility

The challenge is to find a truthful source that operates from some level of accountability for what is published on their website or in their publication. When considering a text's accuracy, they need to integrate the information and avoid plagiarism, which is a tricky topic.

Using Sources

Fifth graders summarize and paraphrase information. 6th graders are asked to quote and paraphrase the data and conclusions of others. Beyond fifth-grade demands, they must extrapolate conclusions from those sources rather than just explain the meaning. In addition, they are charged with avoiding plagiarism, unlike fifth graders.

Citing Sources

The elementary schoolers only provide a list of sources. For the first time, 6th graders need basic bibliographic information for sources. Basic information may be the title of the source, the author, or the date of publication. Later students will need to follow a particular format, known as MLA or APA.

Assessing the credibility

Assessing the credibility of each source is required for informative and argumentative texts. This requirement also includes research projects. Students should be choosing sources that are produced by reputable organizations, colleges, universities, and government entities.

WRITING STANDARD 9 - RESPONSE TO LITERATURE

W 5.9	W 6.9
Draw evidence from literary or informational texts to support analysis, reflection, and research.	Draw evidence from literary or informational texts to support analysis, reflection, and research.

Both 5th and 6th grades call for students to read literary and informational texts. The overall standard is a mirror standard. The standards require students to work on the same skills in both grades. Mastery is not required in fifth grade.

Drawing evidence involves both literary (or narrative texts) and informational texts. Kids will be pulling sentences and phrases from the text in order to integrate it into their writing. Students will use it to support their analysis of a topic, and it will help them to reflect on what they have learned.

Comparing Literary Forms

W 5.9A	W 6.9A
Apply grade 5 reading standards to literature (e.g., "Compare and contrast two or more characters, settings, or events in a story or a drama, drawing on specific details in the text [e.g., "how characters interact]").	Apply grade 6 reading standards to literature (e.g., "Compare and contrast texts in different forms or genres [e.g., stories and poems; historical novels and fantasy stories] in terms of their approaches to similar themes and topics").

Students will read from a range of genres: stories and poems, historical novels, and fantasy stories. Next, they will compare the presentation of similar themes and topics in each text. In fifth grade, students may compare and contrast two or more settings or characters in a narrative. They analyze the different characters, settings, events, and interactions in one story. In the next grade level, this changes to comparisons between different forms or genres.

6th grade requirements scale up in difficulty by asking students to look at two different texts with very similar topics. Middle school students have fun critiquing a movie version of a book they have read. They can decide which form is better, explain aspects missing from the movie contained in the book, and the parts included in the movie that were not part of the book. Students could explain how the missing or added parts altered the message or theme. This can also be done with plays and a novel or comparing a movie versus a play.

Teach this concept with two different works with the same theme. A poem and a letter could both be about how love conquers all. Students need to explain how each genre presents this theme. Historical novels and fantasy stories could also be used.

Response to Literature

5.9B	6.9B
Apply grade 5 Reading standards to informational texts (e.g., "Explain how an author uses reasons and evidence to support particular points in a text, identifying which reasons and evidence support which point[s]").	Apply grade 6 Reading standards to literary nonfiction (e.g., "Trace and evaluate the argument and specific claims in a text, distinguishing claims that are supported by reasons and evidence from claims that are not").

This standard details a new genre of writing not previously discussed, known as response to literature. Reading and writing standards overlap. In this case, children need to write about their readings to demonstrate comprehension. The specific writing prompts can be taken directly from the grade level reading standards as referenced above.

Both fifth grade and sixth grade require responses to an informational text. Sixth grade standards specify literary nonfiction. Literary nonfiction could be a memoir or a biography.

Students need to find more than one point the author is making. Then they should be able to link different reasons and evidence to those specific points that the author is making in the text for fifth grade. The sixth grade standard also uses the terminology argument instead of particular points.

The standard uses the terminology claim, which is not in the fifth-grade standards. A claim means opinion. They should be able to distinguish the claims supported by reasons and evidence from claims that are not.

In certain texts, unsupported claims means the author is inserting their own opinion, and they may not back it up or provide evidence. This standard calls for critical media literacy, in which a text is read and vetted for credibility and sound reasoning.

WRITING STANDARD 10 - BUILDING A WRITING PRACTICE

Range of Writing:

W 5.10	W 6.10
Write routinely over extended time frames (time for research, reflection, and revision) and shorter time frames (a single sitting or a day or two) for a range of discipline-specific tasks, purposes, and audiences.	Write routinely over extended time frames (time for research, reflection, and revision) and shorter time frames (a single sitting or a day or two) for a range of discipline-specific tasks, purposes, and audiences.

For standard ten, the range of writing requires students to engage in writing over extended periods and for different purposes. In other words, these standards refer to building a writing practice. This standard encompasses a variety of tasks and activities that align with the standards. It encourages students to develop their writing skills continuously.

5th and 6th grade have mirror standards. There is no distinction between how they are written in the fifth grade and sixth grades.

CHAPTER 8 REVIEW - ELEMENTARY TO MIDDLE SCHOOL WRITING STANDARDS

This chapter provides a comprehensive exploration of the writing standards, comparing the expectations between fifth and sixth grades. The Common Core State Standards pinpoint crucial differences that mark the transition from elementary to secondary level writing. Understanding these distinctions is vital to ensure your child progresses beyond elementary writing skills and comprehends the demands of the higher grades.

The standards outlined offer specific guidance regarding the genres that educators and parents should focus on teaching explicitly. These genres encompass opinion or argument writing, informative or explanatory pieces, research reports, narratives, and responses to literature.

By gaining a thorough grasp of the disparities between the expectations of 5th and 6th grade writing, parents and teachers are equipped to design lessons and strategies tailored to foster excellence in the upcoming generation of writers. This understanding serves as a solid foundation for constructing effective teaching practices that align with the evolving requirements at the secondary level.

BIBLIOGRAPHY

Access Center. "Teaching Writing to Diverse Student Populations."
Reading Rockets, www.readingrockets.org/topics/writing/articles/
teaching-writing-diverse-student-populations. Accessed 22 Dec.
2023.

Archer, A., & Hughes, C. (2011). Explicit Instruction: Effective and
Efficient Teaching. *New York: Guilford Publications.*

Castagno-Dysart, Dawn, et al. "The Importance of Instructional
Scaffolding." *Teacher Magazine*, 23 Apr. 2019, www.
teachermagazine.com/au_en/articles/the-importance-of-
instructional-scaffolding. Accessed 22 Dec. 2023.

Council Of Chief State School Officers, and National Governors'
Association. Common Core State Standards Initiative . United
States, 2022. Web Archive.

Culham, Ruth. 6 + 1 Traits of Writing: The Complete Guide, Grades 3
and Up. *Scholastic Professional Books*, 2003.

Hebert, Michael, et al. "Why Children with Dyslexia Struggle with
Writing and How to Help Them." *Language, Speech, and Hearing
Services in Schools*, vol. 49, no. 4, 24 Oct. 2018, pp. 843–863,
www.ncbi.nlm.nih.gov/pmc/articles/PMC6430506/, https://doi.
org/10.1044/2018_lshss-dyslc-18-0024.

www.ingramcontent.com/pod-product-compliance
Lightning Source LLC
Chambersburg PA
CBHW070729130626
46553CB00005B/2212